'And we can't get rid of her now no-fault evictions have been scrapped'

THE BEST OF

2023

MATTHEW PRITCHETT

studied at St Martin's School of Art in London and first saw himself published in the *New Statesman* during one of its rare lapses from high seriousness. He has been the *Daily Telegraph*'s front-page pocket cartoonist since 1988. In 1995, 1996, 1999, 2005, 2009 and 2013 he was the winner of the Cartoon Arts Trust Award and in 1991, 2004 and 2006 he was 'What the Papers Say' Cartoonist of the Year. In 1996, 1998, 2000, 2008, 2009, 2018 and 2019 he was the *UK Press* Cartoonist of the Year and in 2015 he was awarded the Journalists' Charity Award. In 2002 he received an MBE.

Own your favourite Matt cartoons. Browse the full range of Matt cartoons and buy online at www.telegraph.co.uk/mattprints or call 0191 6030178.

'He'll do anything to torment the postman. Now he's launching a cyber-attack on the Royal Mail'

The Daily Telegraph

THE BEST OF

MATT

2023

SEVEN DIALS

An Orion Paperback

First published in Great Britain in 2023 by Seven Dials
A division of the Orion Publishing Group Ltd
Carmelite House
50 Victoria Embankment
London
EC4Y 0DZ

An Hachette UK Company

10 9 8 7 6 5 4 3 2 1

A CIP catalogue record for this book is available from the British Library.

ISBN mmp: 978 1 3996 1041 4
ISBN ebook: 978 1 3996 1042 1

Printed in Italy by Elcograf S.p.A.

The Orion Publishing Group's policy is to use papers that are natural,
renewable and recyclable products and made from wood grown in
sustainable forests. The logging and manufacturing processes are expected
to conform to the environmental regulations of the country of origin.

www.orionbooks.co.uk

THE BEST OF
MATT
2023

For Mum

'I'm leaving out a glass of milk and a mince pie in the hope that a train driver might visit on Christmas eve'

'I went into the sorting
office after the 48-hour strike.
There's a dead partridge
in a pear tree'

'I still have a lot of
Christmas presents to buy.
I wonder if the army
would do it for me?'

'Did you call
an ambulance?'

'We've been drafted in
to help during the
ambulance strike'

'Have you thought about what job you'd like to be on strike from?'

'Cheer up, this is the shortest month. There are only 28 strikes in February'

'He's terribly accident prone
and I didn't want him to
injure himself while there's
an ambulance strike'

'Let them pass.
They might be on their
way to a picket line'

'If there's no chance of being taken to hospital in an ambulance, it's hardly worth putting on clean underwear'

'We've found Lord Lucan. He's waiting in an ambulance outside A&E'

'Can I pre-book an ambulance for 1st October? I'm expecting chest pains when I see my new energy bill'

'I'm clapping for the lawyers who stopped next week's NHS strike'

'So, you're going on strike
because your friends are?
And if they jumped off a
cliff would you do that too?'

'Your son is being expelled.
On a strike day he broke
into school, wrote an essay
on Jane Austen, finished
two maths tests and did a
project on the Romans ...'

'We've been fined for taking our children on holiday during an important school strike'

'Dear Education Secretary, Please could my son be excused teaching today as he has a nasty pay offer.'

'Sorry, you were out when Liz Truss tried to deliver, deliver, deliver'

'This is your Tory MP. Forget everything I've said for the past 12 years'

Liz Truss becomes PM

'Goodness knows if it will work, but the shock has completely cured my hiccups'

'Do you want to leave after Liz Truss's speech, or stay for the climbdowns and reversals?'

Mini Budget unravels

Tories

CONSERVATIVES

REVERSING
OUR WAY TO
PROSPERITY

'Liz Truss gave me the
recipe for this cake. If you
change every ingredient,
it's delicious'

'Warning: viewers in
other countries may find
the next item hilarious'

'I'll say one thing for this
new lot – they don't have
many parties'

'Don't bother, they're blowing themselves up'

'I hope Liz Truss isn't forced out this week. I got November 15th in the sweepstake'

'You can see Changing of
the Guard in the morning
and Changing of the
PM most afternoons'

'Are you Conservative Party
members? We try not to give
you a choice because you
always get it wrong'

'Father, when I said I
did not chop down your
cherry tree, technically
that wasn't true...'

'The privileges committee
commissioned this statue
of Boris so that they could
push it into the Thames'

Boris recklessly misled Parliament

'I've decided to vote for
the privileges committee
report, but to tell Boris
that I didn't'

'Imagine you're driving to
a polling station to vote
Labour. When I say "Ulez"
I want you to perform
an emergency stop'

Boris's resignation leads to by-election

Cost of Living Crisis

'The mortgage repayments are bad, but it's the food price inflation that is the real problem'

'DON'T FINISH ALL YOUR VEGETABLES'

'Do you really want to go to
university? For the £9,250
annual fee you could buy a
tub of Lurpak and a chicken'

'The public think the
John Lewis Christmas ad
is a tear-jerker. Wait till they
see the Autumn Statement'

'We don't like the phrase
"Stealing from the rich".
We prefer "Making
difficult decisions"'

'WAIT! I wasn't going to
mention the drought of 1976.
I was going to tell you
about inflation in 1975'

'Apparently, the British have
27 different swear words
for their energy bills'

'This email from a Nigerian
prince looks genuine, but
the £3,549 energy bill
must be a scam'

'It's not good news.
I'm jumping up and
down to keep warm'

'I'm pleased you're all
enjoying our central heating,
but would somebody please
buy a drink?'

'It's full of gas. I'm ready
for energy rationing'

'My husband won't turn the heating on and now David Attenborough is filming Frozen Planet in the hall'

'By 2030 we'll have to change the way we can't afford to heat our home'

'Actually, this is the back of
the queue for Westminster
Hall, in London'

'Judging the right moment
for a joke is always tricky...'

A Nation in Mourning

'48 hours of camping, followed by a five-mile queue. We should get a Duke of Edinburgh award'

Charles's frustration

'Members of the royal
family have superglued
themselves to the road'

'In the Netflix documentary
you're accused of scheming
and you're called a
racist and a bully'

Harry & Meghan repercussions

'If we meet a royal, lead
with the jab, keep your
guard up and watch out
for their left hook'

Harry accuses William
of fighting

'Shortbread biscuits and
Buckingham Palace tea.
Have you tried the
Prince Harry cocaine?'

'*Prince Harry is in the country. This is the Changing Of The Locks*'

Anti-Royal protests

MONARCHS WHO WISH TO BE CROWNED MUST BRING PHOTO ID

'Coronation? I thought this was the queue for an NHS dentist'

'I won't have the fish.
I run a water company;
I know where it's been'

'If you hold this shell to your
ear you can hear the sound
of a flushing loo'

'Pay half and say the rest of
the money leaked away
before it got to them'

'I flushed my A-level results
down the loo. I think
that's them there'

'You become hardened after a while. You wouldn't believe some of the herbaceous borders I've seen'

'Next door's vulture has been in our garden again'

'Would you consider investigating if I told you the burglar watered the garden while he was here?'

'Do you think it's safe to use our disposable barbecue now?'

'It's about your boats.
A migration lawyer is here
from the European Court
of Human Rights'

'We gather you arrived in
the UK from Dunkirk in
a small boat in 1940...'

'For balance, we could get
Suella Braverman to
present Goal Of The Month'

'Freezing temperatures,
snow and travel chaos.
Gary Lineker has compared
it to Stalingrad in 1942-43'

Gary Lineker shares his views

'I'm worried about a
World Cup without alcohol.
I hope I don't discover that
I actually hate football'

'I'm drinking to forget
Qatar's human
rights record'

'If you advance up the pitch in small rubber boats the French won't try to stop you'

'If football is thinking of coming home someone should tell it about the planned Border Force strikes'

'You can't just switch from being a Celtic supporter to a Rangers supporter, son. Sixteen is too young to make such a decision'

'So, you ate grandma and now you want to be sent to a women's prison?'

'At school today a teacher misgendered my imaginary friend'

'Sir, I identify as a dog and I ate my own homework'

'This term your son has identified as a cat. I gave him an F grade because the school still has a mouse problem'

'They take ages to train. When we get them they're not yet sexist, racist or homophobic'

'We can do this the easy way or the hard way, but you will tell us what your pronouns are'

'Just Stop Oil protesters are on the M25. Which motorway should we block to protest against inheritance tax?'

'We know you're boiling an egg. Switch off the gas and put down the timer'

'Bad news, President Putin. Ukrainian forces are advancing by two table-lengths every day'

'Putin is doing a lot of macho posturing. I bet his calendar next year will be a scorcher...'

'Have you recently come
out of retirement, doctor?'

'Hmmm ... let's try a
gin and tonic and see if
there's any improvement'

'My parrot has bird flu'

'It's a phone alert from
the Bank of England:
"YOU'RE ALL POORER"'

'What if Putin attacks the
UK at 3pm on Sunday
when we're all getting a
test alert on our phones?'

'There's an emergency alert on my phone! Do you think Dominic Raab could be in our neighbourhood?'

After Chas Addams

'I didn't get a phone alert. Did you?'

Raab accused of bullying

'The inside of a haggis is like the SNP's finances: it's best not to look too closely'

'Nicola Sturgeon said Westminster is to blame, but she hasn't worked out how'

Scottish Troubles

'I've only been hiding Easter eggs. I know nothing about the SNP's missing £600,000'

'After I've climbed the Scottish Munros I'm going to Edinburgh to scale the mountains of rubbish'

Refuse collectors strike

'If your street had eight potholes last month and 16 this month, how long before the council does something?'

'I'm going for a swim. The council has filled all the potholes with chlorinated water'

'I wanted to crash into the Downing Street gates, but I couldn't afford the petrol, Ulez Charge and Congestion Charge'

'Come quickly, darling. She's doing her first slow protest march!'

'They say AI could kill
humans within two years.
On the plus side, we can
stop worrying about
climate change'

'One day we can get
Artificial Intelligence
to refuse to debate
controversial issues'

'The Chinese won't send a spy balloon to the UK. Our fridge and lightbulbs tell them everything already'

'And this is where we develop the latest top secret spy balloons'

'Gin and tonic. Ice and a slice of turnip?'

'If the DUP MPs back the
Windsor Framework
they'll each get four tonnes
of fresh cucumbers'

'Next, take the Northern
Ireland Protocol and
insert it into Slot A...'

'We've attached the bank to the pen. The pen is worth more'

'Cryptocurrency is finished. I've just bought three billion chocolate coins wrapped in gold foil'

'Oops. I hope that doesn't leak out. I was developing a banking contagion'

'I'll be furious if I discover
that all my husband's
banana bread
was unnecessary'

'It's terrifying how easily
WhatsApp messages can
be passed from
person to person'

Matt Hancock

'I ensure I am socially distanced from my TV whenever Matt Hancock is appearing on it'

'Some people in Whitehall believe that Matt Hancock was developed in a Chinese lab...'

'When it comes to protesting, Brits have a short moan at their desk, while the French take two hours off for a proper riot with tear gas'

French riots

And finally...

'There will be a delay, so
if anyone needs to renew
their passport they
do have time'

'I refer the class to my
essay last year on
airport strikes...'

Book censorship

And finally…

*'The bank of mum and dad
is closing your account.
Your views on getting a job
do not align with ours'*

*'Our special of the day
is locally caught
space rocket debris'*

Virgin rocket crashes

'He's had the miracle
weight-loss injection'

'We went skiing in the Alps,
but there was no snow.
I fell off a sun lounger'

And finally…

'I paid extra for Priority Cancellation. We can give up and go home before the other passengers'

'One of our guests was lightly poached'

Dear Homeowner,
There is a £1,000 fine
for gossiping about the
mystery BBC presenter
without a valid TV licence.

Explicit Photos Scandal

'It's looking serious.
President Putin's body
doubles are getting their
own body doubles'

And finally...

And finally...

Racism in Cricket Report

'Now the river water has really hit the fan'

'If the strike goes well there's talk
of a sequel, a prequel and a range
of merchandise'

'Why don't we just blow
down our own house?'

And finally...

'I bought a petrol car so I can drive round looking for a working charger for my wife's electric vehicle'